Animal Hero's and Miracles
By
Patti Chiappa

Table of Contents

Introduction

It's that magical time of year again. When the world stops spinning for a moment and we breathe a collective sigh as peace reins on Earth and there is good will towards men. They say a dog is a man's best friend, and I totally agree, but I also think that cats, pigs, horses, birds and even snakes can be added to that best friends list. If you are an animal lover like me, you will see the beauty in every animal. As the Holiday Season nears I wanted to take the time to honor the furry angels in our lives for I do not think they get enough credit, after all they have to put up with the biggest animal of all ----- mankind. So let your heart be filled with cheer as you read about the amazing animal heroes in this book. I ask that if you are thinking about getting a dog or cat this Christmas that you save a life--- adopt from a shelter!

Kathy, the Kitty

Kathy came into Paris Harrison's life at a time Paris needed a friend the most. Paris was going through her second divorce, had just lost her job and was now getting ready to move out of state.

Kathy, the kitty was going through a rough time too. She had been abandoned by her previous owner, was living under a bridge and was skin and bones.

Paris feel in love with the stray as soon as she spotted her as she was driving to a friend's house.

Paris worked hard to win over Kathy's trust but when she did, Kathy became a loyal friend.

Paris and Kathy were living together for three weeks, when Paris made her big move from Covington, G.A. TO Memphis , Tenn. On the way to her new home, Paris stopped at a local gas station to put gas in the U-Haul truck she was driving.

As she was at the gas station, Kathy somehow got out of the truck without Paris realizing it. By the time Paris did Kathy was gone!

Fearing that she would never see Kathy again, Paris contacted the local animal shelters and put up flyers in her new town, hoping someone had seen Kathy.

 3 weeks went by. No one had seen Kathy. Paris began to lose hope.

Then one day, Paris' friend from G.A. called all excited. "Paris, you are not going to believe me if I tell you this, but Kathy is sitting on the step of your old house!"

Yes, that's right Kathy, the faithful kitty had traveled over 1000 miles to try to find her lost owner. A week later Paris and Kathy were reunited!

Porkchop, the pig

(Dedicated to my best friend Stevi and her two potbelly pigs Bass and Simone)

My friend Stevi tells me that pigs are much smarter then dogs. As she puts it," they are smarter than some humans too." After hearing about this next hero pig it makes me wonder if Stevi is right.

In a small Iowa town a local farmer by the name of Jake Roberts and his wife Kate live a quiet and simple life. Jake and Kate had been married 43 years when the incident I am about to reveal occurred.

Jake and Kate were getting up in age, but they didn't want to sell their

farm, even though their family and friends showed concern.

Jake, had been a farmer all his life and he was not about to change now.

On May 28, 2008, Jake and Kate's life changed forever. In the small town of Parkersburg, an Ef5 tornado ripped the town to sherds. Jake and Kate's farm was hit hard. Very hard.

Kate and Jake were trapped in their farm house. They didn't think they would live to see another sunrise. They thought all their animals were dead, which most of them were. But a sweet pot belly pig named Pork chop had survived.

You see Kate and Jake were not supposed to be home that Memorial

Weekend. They were supposed to be visiting their grandchildren in Ohio. But they cancelled the trip at the last minute because Kate was coming down with a cold. So none of their friends in the area knew that they were trapped.

Kate had a broken hip. She was trapped over part off the roof. Jake had a broken back.

They tried screaming for help, but their frail voices gave out within a few hours.

But Porkchop knew that her owners needed help!

So Porkchop found the courage to walk 3 miles with a broken tail and bruises all over her. She stood on the nearest neiborger's porch squealing until he came outside to see what was making all that noise.

Frank Dwight, age 62 recognized Porkchop. His house was untouched but all around him there was rubble.

He was surprised to see Porkchop had lived through the storm. When Frank saw Porkchop , he got the awful feeling that something was terribly wrong.

You see Porkchop was running back and forth trying to get Frank to follow her to her owner's farm.

Frank loaded Porkchop up in his pick-up truck and headed to Kate and Jake's farm.

When he got there, he was heartbroken. The house and barn had been leveled. There was nothing left.

Frank began looking around to see if any of the other animals had survived, because he knew Jake and his wife were away, well at least that is what he thought!

As he began to search, Frank found a cow that had survived. But then from the house he heard a faint sound. "Help us." The voice called out. My God it was Kate!

Frank rushed to get some help, while faithful Porkchop looked after the wounded cow and her wounded owners.

When Frank came back with help, he and the rescues workers saw an unforgettable sight!

Porkchop was trying to move the rubble with her snout! The hero pig, had saved her owners life. Both Kate and Jake recovered!

Alice, the bunny

When you think of bunnies, a watch bunny doesn't really seem to fit. Most bunnies are fluffy and cuddly. But not Alice!

Brentwood, New York. Lisa Whitestone adopted Alice from a local pet store. Lisa had always loved bunnies and her favorite book was Alice in Wonderland so it was natural for Lisa to name her new friend Alice.

Lisa, a hard-working college student had just moved into her very first Apartment. Lisa was excited to be starting a new chapter in her life.

But little did she know danger was lurking in the shadows. One Saturday night Lisa, who worked nights came home in the wee-hours of the morning after working her shift at a Local White Castle.

She came home to find her apartment had been broken into. Frightened to death, Lisa quickly dialed 911. When the police arrived they found a curious thing. Alice was out of her cage. And she had blood around her mouth.

Lisa, afraid that the robber had hurt Alice inspected Alice to find that Alice was not the one that was hurt. Alice had bit the robber.

Taking a sample of blood that had dried around Alice's mouth, police were able to I.D. the low-life who

broke into Lisa's home. Way to go Alice!

Winter, the dolphin

Some of you may have heard the story of Winter. The sweet baby dolphin who almost died after losing her tail, the star of Dolphin Tale the movie, but did you also know that Winter is a real life hero?

Not just because she fought her way back from the grip of death. No you see Winter is now helping disabled children and Vets that have been injured in the wars. She has become a true inspiration.

Winter is helping amputees in other ways also. You see the doctor who created Winter's new tail is applying that same since to building new limbs for amputees.

A dog named Dog

When two year old, Harriet Livenstein and her mother Missy went to the local animal shelter to adopt a new puppy, they never realized they were adopting a hero.

Harriet, had been born with heart defects. Missy didn't know how long she would have Harriet, so she wanted to give her a full and happy life for as long as she had her.

What Harriet wanted the most was a puppy.

So Missy brought her little angel to adopt one. Harriet feel in love with a black and brown female lab mix she named," Dog."

Dog was a gentle and loving soul. She was the perfect match for little Harriet.

Dog, was amazing. She trained herself to be housebroken, seemed to sense when Harriet needed her, and keep a watchful Eye on Missy as well.

One night, Missy and Harriet feel victims to carbon monoxide poisoning.

Dog had trained herself to use the phone. Dog pressed 1 on the speed dial, the number was linked to 911.

When the 911 operator asked where the emergency was, all she heard was dog barking. She was able to trace the address and saved Missy and Harriet before they died.

Dog received a hero's medal from the local police and a life time supply of treats from Missy!

Johnny, the snake

Most people are afraid of snakes. I am one of those people. But for a man in Illinois, a snake named Johnny, has become his hero!

You see, Robert Hinds was hunting when he was nearly killed by a bear, but a rattle snake, yes a rattle snake came along and chased the bear away.

Robert, a professional hunter credits Johnny for saving his life.

"He came out of nowhere, The bear I mean. He began biting me all over. Then all of a sudden I saw this thing crawling on the ground. A snake. A rattlesnake. I said to myself, "S***, I am going to die either by the claws of this bear or by bite of the snake. " Suddenly, the snake passes me right up. He starts attacking this bear! So much so the bear runs off and leaves me alone. Crawling on the ground bleeding, I am thinking this snake is going to bite me. But he doesn't. He just kind of looks at me and crawls off!"

Johnny, the snake is now being used by scientists for his life-saving venom.

Leo, the elephant

Leo, was a retired circus elephant living in India. His handler was an older man by the name of Dhamn, meaning blessed one, and Dhamn was blessed that was for sure.

Leo, a 40 year old Elephant loved his owner very much. His owner used to let the children ride him for a small fee to make ends meet. Leo, was a gentle giant.

One day, a huge storm came to the small village where Leo and Dhamn lived.

The village was made up of houses made of mud and straw. Because the village was a very poor one.

The rain came, and the wind. It rained and rained for four days and four nights straight. Then tragic events struck the village, there was a major mud-slide. People were trapped including Dhamn!

Leo, escaped from the area he was kept in unharmed. Sensing that his owner was in danger, Leo slowly began to move pieces of the buildings that had been torn apart by the mudslide. Leo single-handedly saved 5 people including his owner.

In 1983, Leo was honored with a statue that can be found in the small village of Adyar.

Leo died in 1985. His owner Dhamn died two years later.

Millie, the pony

In the middle of the night on a small farm, a colt has been born but is barely clinging to life. The colt has been named Millie. Her mother has just died giving birth to her. Millie is premature.

She is underweight. Joyce and Rhonda Delit sisters and co-owners of the farm keep a 24 hour Virgil for Millie. If she survives the 24 hours, she just might have a fighting chance.

Miraculously, Millie survives. But Millie never grows strong enough to be a work horse. The sisters feel pity for Millie so they keep her.

Millie, turns out to be a living miracle for many.

Millie's owners notice Millie's gentle nature. She seems to be grateful just to be alive. She is a friendly horse.

So Joyce approaches her sister about an idea. "What if we open up the farm in the summer to disabled children? I think Millie will make a great therapy pony." Joyce said. Rhonda agreed to try out the idea.

The summer of 1993, the sisters opened the farm to disabled children but what they witnessed was a true Miracle.

Kevin Ren, an 11 year old boy who had never spoken in his life because he suffered with Autism Spectrum

Disorder started talking when he started to ride Millie.

His mother Diane credits Millie for changing her son's life." I couldn't believe it. Millie opened up an entire new world for Kevin. He started speaking in single words something he could never do before."

Kevin's not the only one that has been affected by Millie's love and care. Five other children and one adult has seen improvement since riding Millie, the wonder horse.

30

Stubby

If you haven't heard of a little dog named Stubby well then you are simply not a history buff.

Stubby was a solider. During ww1. Seriously. Stubby did his part by providing morale-lifting visits up and down the line and occasional early warning about gas attacks or by waking a sleeping sentry to alert him to a German attack.

Stubby was a member of the 102nd Infantry.

STUBBY was also gassed a few times and eventually ended up in a hospital when his master, Corporal J. Robert Conroy, was wounded. After doing hospital duty for a while he and

Conroy returned to the 102nd and spent the remainder of the war with that unit. STUBBY was smuggled back home in much the same way as he entered the War, although by this time he was so well known that you have to suspect that one or two general officers probably looked the other way as he went aboard ship to sail home and muster out with the rest of the regiment.

Back home he became the rock star of dogs! He won many awards including a purple heart!

In 1926 STUBBY finally passed on.

His remains were preserved and presented for display purposes to the Smithsonian. Now that's a real hero.

Thank you for your service to the red, white and blue Stubby.

Noah, the dog that sees with his heart

Noah, a white Bichon-Poodle mix was born without eyes but that doesn't make him any less special! You see sweet little Noah is an anti-bullying advocate.

A local Wisconsin school was having a serve issues with bullying. So the school called upon Noah to help.

"The kids visit with Noah and suddenly, they understand that beauty is not seen with the eyes but with the heart." Say's Noah's owner Lisa. The local schools are crediting Noah as a hero because the bullying issues that were having vanished with Noah's visits.

Noah has won the Emerging Hero Dog Award at the American Humane Associations Hero Dog Awards. Way to go Noah, way to go!

Lassie saves his best friend

Lassie, a four year old German Shepard mix is the hero for a two-year-old chow.

Lassie, a dog from Orange, Massachusetts and his pal Midnight, got loose when their owner had a medical emergency and had to be transported to the Hospital.

One of the officers on the scene, searched for Lassie and Midnight. A few hours later, he spotted Lassie.

Lassie began to bark wildly. So the officer followed Lassie down a steep embankment.

It was then he notice Midnight, had slide down the embankment (about 30 feet) and was trapped on a patch of ice. The officer called the Fire Dept. The fire Dept. rescued Midnight and the two best friends were reunited.

Major Tom saves the day!

A cat that loves water is very rare, But Rod Mcdowel, a man from Melbourne, Australia is thanking God that his cat Major Tom has a love for boating.

46 year old, Mcdowel fell asleep while boating. His cat Major Tom began head-butting him until he awoke.

When Mcdowel awoke he noticed that his 40 foot boat the "Osprey" was filling up with water!

Mcdowel and his cat quickly loaded onto to a life raft where they were saved by a passing ship!

Mcdowel who lived on the boat lost everything but his cat.

Isis, the Pitbull with a big heart.

Pitbull's, for the most part have a bad reputation of being aggressive. So much so that some towns have banned them. That was the case for the town of Hazel Park, Michigan.

Isis, a four year old Pitbull was the hero in a domestic dispute. Jamie Kraczkowski, Isis owner said that the dog saved her from her abusive boyfriend.

Jamie's boyfriend had beaten Jamie so badly that she was left unconscious. But Isis didn't attack Jamie's boyfriend. Instead she dragged Jamie outside to safety and then alerted a nearby cop that was writing parking tickets that Jamie needed help.

Officer Daton reported in his own words," The dog, gently took my arm and lead me to her owner. Once I called for help, Isis then lead me inside the house where Jamie's boyfriend was still hiding. I have never seen anything like it."

Jamie is recovering. Her boyfriend goes to trial in July 2016.

Hazel Park, Michigan has since lifted the ban on pitbulls.

Sissy and Barney friends till the end

This next story made me weep for it reminded me of my dog Smokey.(More about Smokey later)

In Iowa a Miniature Schnauzer by the name of Barney has vanished, after one of his owners Dale Franck has taken him for a walk.

Dale reports that he had just taken Barney for his nightly walk. He let him out into the backyard to play, and Dale went into make himself a cup of coffee, and suddenly he noticed that it was very quiet outside. When he went to search the yard, Barney was gone.

Panic, Dale started walking around looking for Barney but he couldn't find him. It was around midnight when a broken Dale returned home with Barney.

The next morning around 4am, Sissy, Dale's wife called from the Hospital. Sissy was there being treated for complications from a cancer-related surgery.

Her room was on the first floor facing the parking lot. At about 3am, she heard barking at her window. At first she thought she was dreaming, so she called a nurse to check things out.

Sissy's faithful dog Barney had made it all the way to the hospital 20 miles away, even though he had never been there before.

Sissy explains," He had never spent a day without me, so I guess he had to some visit. My little amazing dog. My hero. My friend."

Now for my dog. I got my dog Smokey when he was just a tiny little thing. I don't even think he was six weeks old. It was Easter Sunday. My husband and I ran up to Walmart to grab a couple of things we needed. This lady walked up to us in the parking lot. She had Smokey in this little tiny box. You can barely see the poor little thing. She said, "I am trying to find this little guy a home. He was born under my porch. He is the runt of the litter. No one wants him."

My husband and I feel in love with Smokey. We brought him home. To this day, we don't know honestly what kind of dog he is, but he has become a blessing and angel to me.

You see back in 2011, I had to strokes, right after the strokes a tumor was found in my right leg and on top of that I was diagnosed with the crippling illness of Lupus.

Most of the time, I can't do things on my own. I can't even go to the bathroom by myself.

Since my mobility is very limited, Smokey , my little angel has took it upon himself to become my service dog. No lie. He was never trained to be one. One day, I was home alone and I was struggling to get up from a chair so I could use the bathroom. I was in tears because I couldn't get up. Smokey came running to my side(and I am a big gal) and put my hand gently in his mouth and pulled me up.

He alerts my mom and Husband if I about to get sick. He also stands by my side if I am losing my balance!

He is really man's best friend!

Smokey, my dog who trained himself to be my service dog!

Labrador retriever saves a drowning dog

It was the middle of winter. The temps were below zero. In Andalusia, Iowa, a water treatment plant worker was returning from his lunch break. When a black lab approached him. The lab was desperately trying to gain the man's attention. He began barking and pulling on the man's shirt.

The man followed the dog to see what was the matter. The man notices that another dog is trapped in the below freezing waters trying desperately to get out.

The man quickly dialed 911 from his cell phone.

Police arrived. Not knowing how they would rescue the dog from the icy waters, another officer called a friend who had a boat.

The officer's friend brought the boat to where the dog was trapped and rescued him. The water treatment worker has since adopted both dogs that was abandoned by their former owner.

9/11 HERO DOG

Sept 11,2001 is a day the world will never forget. And for me, a New Yorker by birth it is a day that lives in my nightmares. We all know what happened on 9/11. We also know there were many human heroes that day, but I would like to tell you about a four legged one.

Bretagne, a Golden Retriever is a living legend. Bretagne was deployed to the Ground Zero site as part of FEMA's Urban Search and Rescue group Texas Task Force 1 with her handler, Denise Corliss. They were a relief team, arriving 10 days after the tragedy.

After her time at Ground Zero, Bretagne went on to work at the 2002 Winter Olympics in Salt Lake City and in the aftermath of Hurricane Rita in 2005.

Sadly, she and another dog by the name of Otto who now lives in New Jersey are the only living rescue dog's left living since the 9.11 attacks. Nearly 100 other search and rescue dogs have died of cancer steaming from the 9/11 attacks. I wish I knew the names of them all so I could honor each and every one of them but sadly I don't. Let' us please never forget them as well.

Footnote: Sadly as this book went to print, I found out from a friend of

mine that Bretagne and Otto have died. This means all the search and rescue dogs from 9/11 are sadly gone.

Willie the Quaker parrot

Willie the Quaker was a parrot that lived in Denver loved to clown around. He called himself, "Silly Willie", sang the song to Andy Griffith Show and he liked to mimic the dog.

But in 2006, Willie became a hero.

Samantha Kuusk, her two year old daughter Hannah and another roommate all lived together. Samantha, a college student left to go to class and left her roommate babysitting her daughter.

Meagan Howard, the babysitter sat the little girl in front of the T.V. eating a pop-tart.

Meagan Howard walked into the Kitchen to make breakfast for herself when she heard Willie the Quaker squawk, "Mama Baby "over and over again.

Hannah had started chocking on the pop tart when Willie realized what was happening he called out to the babysitter for help. Thankfully Hannah was fine. And as for Willie, he gets a cracker anytime he wants.

The Lion's den

When you think of Lions you don't really think of cuddly and sweet, but when you read this next story you might think twice.

In 1996 a 13 year old girl who had been kidnapped was saved by not one but three lions!

It is true. It happened in Kenya. A group of men had the kidnapped the girl as she walking to school. The men planned to sell her into human trafficking. But those men got the shock of their life when a family of lions approached the camp where the men were keeping the girl tied. The men went running for their lives, and the girl was found a week later

unharmed being surrounded by the lions!

Brookfield Zoo in Illinois

In Brookfield Zoo in Illinois a little three year old boy falls into a pit with gorillas. The 18 foot drop left the boy with serious life-threating injuries. Because gorillas are dangerously aggressive, Police could not take action right away.

So, with a child in need and no help in sight, Binti Jua stepped in. And as much as that sounds like Indian Superman, it wasn't. Binti just happened to be one of the zoo's gorillas.

Binti came to the boy's aid by cradling him in her arms and then bringing him to the enclosure door, where paramedics could get to him.

The police and staff were quick to note that without Binti's assistance, the situation could have been much worse.

Dolphins save Lifeguards!

In 2004, four lifeguards were swimming off the coast of New Zealand when a pod of dolphins surrounded them underwater.

One of the dolphins jumped out of the water and surfaced in the direction of a 10-foot-long great white shark. As the shark caught sight of the lifeguards, he darted for them, but the dolphins started swimming in a frenzy, blocking his way. The dolphins swam around for close to 40 minutes like this, while the lifeguards got to safety.

Dog saves family and cat from Fire.

Maxie Blue, a Doberman Pincher from New Jersey is the hero for a family of six and a cat named Lucy.

The Smith family, had just adopted Maxie Blue who was found on their steps during a thunder storm.

The poor old dog was so grateful that he risked his own life saving the family from a fire.

It was a Saturday night, New Year's Eve. The family had just gone to bed about an hour before.

Suddenly the Smith Family heard Maxie Blue barking wildly and scratching at their bedroom doors.

When they went to investage they saw flames in the Kitchen. The family's fire alarms had not worked but Maxie saved the lives of all members of her family. Maxie Blue even received second degree burns because she went back inside the burning house to save Lucy, the cat.

Cluck, Cluck the Chicken

On December 28, Cluck Cluck, a chicken saved a Wisconsin couple from a fire. Yes, really, a chicken! Dennis Murawska, 59, said Cluck Cluck woke his wife at about 6:15 am when it made loud clucking noises from its cage in the basement two floors below.

The couple got out just in time, and firefighters were able to save the chicken. Jeff Gaede, the fire chief in Alma Center, was amazed when he discovered that a hero chicken had saved the day. It turns out that Cluck Cluck began wandering over to the Murawaska home from a nearby farm a while ago. The chicken had a mutated foot, and Cluck Cluck's owner had declared his intention to kill the bird because it wasn't producing any eggs. That's when Murawska made up his mind to save the chicken, a decision that really paid off for him!

Ellie The Donkey

Ellie is credited with saving three horses and another donkey from Colorado's High Park wildfire after the couple boarding them was forced to evacuate. The animals could not be reached for evacuation before the fire moved through their area and were feared lost, but a rescue crew sweeping the area after the fire discovered the herd in a safe place, with Ellie in charge.

It was Ellie who had moved them all to one of the few remaining unburned areas. Overall the horses and donkeys in Ellie's care weathered the fire without any serious injuries.

Ellie's nose and coat were singed by the flames, but didn't need any treatment. The tails of the four horses had curled from the extreme heat.There were a few singed whiskers and tails, but everyone survived, and when Ellie climbed into the rescue crew's horse trailer, the herd followed her as they had before.

Hooray for Ellie and all of these amazing animals!

The bear who saved a man

California hiker Robert Biggs was exploring the Whiskey Flats when he found a few bears drinking near a stream. Out of nowhere, a mountain lion leaped on him, knocking the man down and biting his arm. The bears quickly came to his aid and fought off the mountain lion, saving Biggs' life.